A Journey Through Recovery

A special thank you to Dave and Tom for guiding me through the frustrations of computer graphics while helping to improve my computer literacy.

Thank you to all my brothers and sisters who have encouraged and nurtured my creativity and gave me the strength to complete this project

Thank you to my wife and daughter for being patient.

A Journey Through Recovery

*Poems about growing,
changing, and
learning to live*

ANDRE P. LAVIGNE

Orangua Publishing

Waterford, New York

Published by Orangua Publishing
52 Fourth Street, Waterford, New York 12188

The Orangua Publishing logo is copyrighted
by Orangua Publishing

ISBN 0-9662815-0-0
Library of Congress Catalog Number 98-091281
Copyright © 1996, by Orangua Publishing
PRINTED IN THE UNITED STATES OF AMERICA

DEDICATION

This book of poetry is dedicated to both my immediate and extended families.

To my wife, Jean, and my daughter, Karen, who have both grown in so many wonderful ways.

To my son, Kenneth, who was never able to experience the joy and sadness of life.

To my son, Michael, and the other unfortunate souls who were not able to experience the fullness of living.

To the many recovering individuals who have helped to guide me in my journey.

TABLE OF CONTENTS

TEARDROPS

As miniature falls cascade
   to crystal pools below
Teardrops silently ease
   down my face ever slow
Each brings a sadness or joy
   about a part of my past
Each brings a memory gone by
   that just would not last
As these mirrors of life
   reflect all my fears
I'll forget what I've done
   and shed no more tears.

THE ELUSIVE DREAM

I try to think
    through clouded mind
        about solutions
            that I could find;

About what is right
    and just for me,
        to set my life
            forever free.

Then through the clouds
    and hazy mist
        my soul is caressed
            and gently kissed.

I'll grow with passion
    from this tiny seed,
        and find my path
            to what I need.

It's love of self
    I need the most;
        to be a comforting
            and gentle host.

I'll nurture the child
    I carry inside;
        I'll set him free;
            I'll be his guide.

He'll rise above
    this earthly hell —
        a loving being
            not afraid to tell

Of the anger and hurt,
　　that's in his heart
　　　　for loved ones near
　　　　　　or far apart.

But the grip of the past
　　is impossible to break.
　　　　The ache is so intense
　　　　　　its hard to take.

You exist in days,
　　dreading the nights;
　　　　forever struggling
　　　　　　for the glow of lights

That guide the soul
　　down shady a lane;
　　　　hiding the doubt
　　　　　　and easing its pain.

Someday I'll be free
　　and calmly content.
　　　　I'll sleep in the peace
　　　　　　that God has sent.

REFLECTIONS OF YESTERDAY

I look toward new horizons
    to find what's right for me
And dream of what I wish I was
    and who I want to be.
To be free of all the trouble
    and guilt from times before;
To rid myself of all my grief
    and live my life for evermore.

Behind the sky is gray and bleak,
    the clouds are filled with rain;
Just like the life I had before
    filled with hidden pain.
Though very few can comprehend
    the peace that I have found;
My days are filled with love again
    I'm aware of the world around.

Though I hide among the masses,
    I stand out in the crowd;
I long for peace and quiet
    while crying ever loud;
I long to be different
    yet I try just like all the rest;
To be content with what I was,
    still trying to be the best.

And now it doesn't matter
    that things don't go my way.
I take life as it comes along
    each and every day.
I don't care what others think;
    no matter what they see
It makes me happy and serene;
    makes me feel free!

THE CIRCLE

The circle folded over many times,
yet the continuity remained.
Within each fold lies a principle,
a small fragment of recovery.
The circle unfolds,
the fragments separate,
the strength grows.

the hole of life

i looked into the emptiness
into a hole so deep and black
once i'd reach the bottom
i knew i could not come back
then the ledge began to crumble
and down i began to fall
my voice was ever silent
for help i could not call

the light began to vanish
further from my view
i knew my life had ended
there was nothing i could do
if only i could pray a little
my voice might just be heard
but silently i fell some more
i could not say a word

i wished I'd reach the bottom
no more to descend
but i guess i'll just keep on
falling and never meet my end!

LAUGHING

I laughed a little but cried a lot
    not so long ago
The pain filled each tiny pore
    and dimmed my golden glow

My ship was cast upon the sea
    and pushed from side to side
And every reef that crashed the hull
    crushed my foolish pride

Billowing clouds filled the sky
    and blocked the shining sun
My life was filled with sadness
    there was just no time for fun

Suddenly the storm subsided
    the wind faded to a hush
I watched the world from a different view
    Slowly — now I would not rush

And now I cry a little
    but laugh a whole lot more
I'm better now! I've learned a lot,
    more than I knew before!

BREAKING FREE

I sit and look around
 at where I am right now;
I dread I'll be here tomorrow
 so I take this solemn vow:

That somehow, some way, some time
 I'll escape this self-made prison.
To seek a truer, newer life,
 and chase my lifelong vision.

I'll live my life in freedom,
 accepting what is in my way
Trusting that it will all work out
 and I'll find happiness each day

I'll muster all my courage,
 to change my life around;
Though life is still so hectic
 I'll relish the quiet that I've found.

This silence will fill my soul;
 as I live my days in peace.
Each moment will bring me happiness;
 my passion will increase.

My love of life and love of self
 are something I never knew;
No friends to share my troubles
 or help in what I do.

And, yet, I still just sit around
 and try to do what's right;
I hang my head in such despair
 shackled by this lonely plight.

THE JOYS OF RECOVERING YOUTH

They envelope the rooms
    like a surf covers the shore
A gentle, distant murmur
    growing to a mighty roar
A lonely flying bird
    hovering high above
Seeking for a home
    to fill with all its love
The pain of a silent hell
    grips each tortured being
Still they search daily
    afraid of what they're seeing.
So young and yet so old
    they've hurt more than most
They've cried each night alone
    haunted by unknown ghosts

Now there's hope, they've found the strength
    to conquer all their fears
To live a life filled with joy
    that will last throughout the years
Together, as one, their strength will grow
    and protect each fragile mind
They'll cope with all that life will give
    no matter what they find
Such is the power of youth
    who want to be something more
Who want to pass from inner darkness
    to bask in sunlight by the shore

LIVING FROM DAY TO DAY

If only we had a little time,
    to sit silently alone,
We'd find our life rewarding;
    for our sins we could atone
We'd admit to all our ignorance
    of life outside our mind.
We'd realize just what we missed
    though we tried so hard to find.
We'd discover each common pleasure
    just outside our door;
We'd bring them in, into our hearts,
    and keep them there forevermore.

But such is not what can be done,
    for life runs not this way.
We rush around from place to place;
    we're busy throughout the day.
We bask in each success,
    we must be best in all we do.
We must climb up to the very top.
    "I " must be better than "You"

Alas, our plight is chosen;
    nothing can be done.
We're doomed to vile frustration;
    there's just no time for fun.
No time to enjoy the things that God
    has placed upon this earth.
We must live our lives dejected —
    lifeless, without joy or mirth.
And so the tale is sounded
    to all who follow me;
Just live your life day by day
    just dream of being free.

REVEL IN HIS POWER

As the sadness draws near
And your thoughts become gray
May He protect you from fear
For this I will pray.

May He fill you with grace
And protect you from harm
As you lay down in place
Cradled in His arm.

May the strength of His might
Fill you with hope
As He protects you each night
And helps you to cope.

Put your trust in a Power
From somewhere above
And revel in the shower
Of His everlasting love.

A MAN'S VOICE WITHIN

We listened to the voices
        they came from deep within
Be gentle, loving, caring
        I know you did not sin
You were not such a bad child
        as you grew to be a man
You had some misconceptions
        you did not understand
You tried to love but couldn't
        no one showed you how
The love was locked within your heart
        that is, until now
For at this very moment
        your blessings you can see
We love as men together
        to be whatever we can be

THE LAKE

I looked across the water
    for now it was very still
The daytime sky darkened
    and the water began to chill
My life passed before my eyes
    I like not what I did
Ever since I began to grow
    from a lonely little kid
The biting wind began to blow
    and the lake began to churn
As my life flashed on by
    with lessons I had to learn
The lonely night passed on by
    and I saw the morning light
My soul felt relief again
    as the sun came into sight

VISION QUEST

I scaled to the top of a mountain
    and searched my soul for truth
And looking down to a lake below
    there I was, a lonely youth
I floundered aimlessly
    not knowing what to do
While a haze of clouds floated lazily
    cast in grayish hue
I flailed my arms and tried in vain
    to stop from sinking deep
Not finding truth had brought me sadness
    yet still, I could not weep
I tried so hard to keep afloat
    though I didn't really care
The time had come to change my life
    but still I could not dare
The water with its chill at night
    and warmth throughout the day
Will keep me safe throughout my life
    when I know not what to say
And when I tire and slip down under
    the lake of crystal blue
My life would be serene at last
    with nothing more to do
Then through the water a golden light
    brightened my clouded mind
My soul swelled with the real truth
    I was trying so hard to find.

ITS JUST ENOUGH

I'm happy while walking alone;
I'm awed by the falling of leaves.
I'm content to be silent and listen
to the birds as they play in the
tops of the trees.

But I do not feel overwhelmed,
fulfilled and ecstatic beyond belief.

I like the closeness of the friends
I've made through life who help me
through the day; who bring some light
into my blackness that's turned from
gloomy gray.

But my heart feels heavy, empty —
laden with so much grief.

I wish I could feel happiness as it
drifts across my mind, lifting me
from despair; bringing me from the
edge of nothingness; helping me to
care.

Though all these things make me
happy, they just aren't enough; they
give me no satisfaction; they give me
no relief.

OBSTACLES

I stand before my brothers shrouded
in a storm of recovery; content to
seek my identity, as a man but unable
to do so. Longingly, I trudge down
the trail of fulfillment only to veer
right or left when obstacles confront
me. I lose myself in the briars on the
right. I struggle in pain seeking a way
out. To the left I fall endlessly downward.
And when, luckily, I reach bottom I begin to
claw upward toward the light.

I may be able to avoid the obstacles
but they will soon reappear somewhere
down the road. Unless I can crash through
them and overcome their pull I shall never
be free. I will never be able to find myself;
I shall never discover the real man inside;
never feel happiness; never enjoy each day,
never be me. They will forever overshadow my
life, binding me to the past, sheltering me
from the future, masking the present.

THE REALITIES OF LIFE

Every single day is spent
    doing what you have to do,
Trying what you have to try,
    learning what you have to learn;

      Delving deep into your mind,
        finding all that's truly true,
      Putting in a day of work,
        earning what you have to earn.

And each defeat is but a spot,
    a blemish on a worthless life,
A stain upon your swollen pride,
    a pain to hound your feeble mind.

      New problems loom around each bend
        and fill your work with bitter strife.
      You look and search wherever you can
        for solutions you just can't find.

And so it goes throughout the year,
    month by month and day by day.
You trudge along and do your job;
    doing the best you can somehow.

      This day will linger, but it will pass;
        you hope to accomplish something today.
      The things you've set yourself to do,
        that must be done right here, right now!

GROWING AS ONE

Two silhouettes share the
sunlight; vague outlines in the
morning; shadows of who they
really are.

As the sun rises the faces appear;
the hands can be seen clasped;
entwined as one, together.

Slowly, there is love in their eyes;
the fingers gently caressing;
silently, exploring their real
selves.

Suddenly, they are distinct;
two separate beings apart;
boundaries between the "I's"

The moon casts its pale glow
and the shadows reappear;
together they live,
      together they love!

STINGING TEARDROPS

Raindrops sting
My barren flesh and
Scar my weakened soul
Dampness seeps
Into my being and
Chills a lifeless heart
The downpour blurs
The landscape and
Fills me with nothingness
The monotonous rain
Reminds me of my life
And the ever-present
emptiness!

A RAINY DAY

The way ahead is dreary and gray;
The rain pelts the land frantically.
The sky above is hidden by the clouds;
There is no sun, no joy, no hope —
Only sadness and sorrow surrounds me.

How long will the darkness last?
When will the blackness turn to light?
When will the sun dry the dampness?
When will new growth sprout forth?
When will there be a sense of happiness?

The loneliness seems forever;
Yet there is no desire for togetherness.
The shrouded thoughts linger;
Yet there is no desire for enlightenment.
Life is but a grasp away;
Yet there is no desire to live.

TEARDROPS FROM HEAVEN

There is no joy down here below
the dark and dreary sky. The
days pass by so slowly as God
began to cry. He cried for all
his people who've lived their
lives in sin. He cried for all
who tried so hard but could not
seem to win. He cried for all
the sorrow that fills each
lonely heart. He cried when
two loved ones seemed so far
apart. He cried each time a
long lost soul found his chosen
road. He cried each time a
cherished friend shared another's
load. He cried each time the clock
struck nine and people prayed
aloud. He cried each time a
friendly face was seen among
a crowd. He cried when people
died and left behind a friend.
He cried throughout their life
of woe right up to the end. Yes,
God cries just like we do. He's
saddened just like us. But he
knows that life is better, if only
we could trust.

WHERE IS LOVE?

Where is love? Did I lose it yesterday?
Will I find it today and give it tomorrow?
Will I embrace you and let you in
Will I tell you what I feel, what I want, who I am?
Will I expose my fears, my needs, my desires?
Will I feel comfortable being with you?
Will I feel comfortable being with me?

I've searched for love forever.
Deeper and deeper I've delved; winding
Through the bowels of my recovery
Endlessly circling this way and that;
Searching, endlessly searching; losing
Myself in the maze. Burying my soul,
Entombing my spirit; wallowing in the
Molten fluidity of despair.

It lurks always just beyond my grasp,
Sometimes resting in my head but never
In my heart.
  Testing me.
    Teasing me.
      Tormenting me.
Laughing at me in my sadness;
  Rejoicing in my despair and filling
    Me with emptiness.

Alone with myself, unable to give;
Love flits by and leaves for now until
It comes again to haunt me.

TURMOIL OF LIFE

I go to church and search my soul,
    "What have I done so bad?"
To deserve the grief that's come my way,
    the troubles I've always had.
I think about the days I've done
    about everything I could.
I've tried so very hard,
    to do what I thought I should.
I've tried to help my loved ones
    live a richer, fuller life;
To be father to my children
    and husband to my wife.
And, yet, nothing seems enough,
    everything I've done I've failed.
My life has been a prison cell;
    forever have I been jailed.
I hear of others around me
    who discover that peace of mind
That helps them through this crisis
    to leave their past behind.
My mind is in a quandary,
    "What is wrong and what is right?"
I wish that I could find the path;
    I wish that I could see the light.

YEARNINGS

Another day passes by
      slowly creeps before my eye
I watch and look and hope to see
      something, anything, new to me
Alas, there's nothing new to view
      only jobs I have to do
An endless maze of pure frustration
      brings only monotonous devastation
Each hour lingers; slow, so slow,
      with days on top and minutes below

It's time to find a new desire
      to raise my dreams ever higher
To raise my soul from Satan's den
      shake this lousy mood, and then,
To come alive, free from pain
      to live my life over again
To sigh a sigh of deep relief
      to free myself from hidden grief
I've cleared my mind from evil thought
      my life again is not for naught
A meaning is there in all I do
      I love someone, she loves me too

This is a dream, a fantasy of mind.
      this kind of life I'll never find
There's nothing new that lies ahead
      nothing worthy of being said
This world degenerates all too fast
      desired life is in the past
This past is gone! There's no rebirth!
      its buried deep within this earth
From this earth your life is given
      back to dirt you must be driven.

CATCHING THE SUNLIGHT

Catch hold of the sunlight as it brightens
the earth. Let it fill your heart with a
sense of worth. Let its light guide your
way from the depths of despair and give
you strength to do what you could not dare.
Let its warmth heal the wounds, that have
caused you so much pain; and let it bring
you self-esteem and make you whole again.

CONFUSION - THE ENDLESS SEARCH

Life is but a time on earth
    filled with lots of pain
Each time I see the light above
    The sky fills up with rain
It falls to earth so heavy
    with a thunderous, chilly thud
And turns green fields of splendor
    into pools of dirty mud
I know not why my time on earth
    has been the way it's been
Is life this depressing
    for all the other men?
I try to work to better
    this lowly, worthless soul
And learn what I'm supposed to do
    to define my future role
But I doubt the very essence
    of what I did before
I question my every action
    and wish I'd done so much more
For years I felt so godly
    only I could do what's right
To correct the wrongs of mankind
    I fought a hopeless fight
I thought I could change the world
    and make a better place to live
I did my all for everyone
    and gave all that I could give

I can't get it through my head
    that there's happiness somewhere
I've never really felt for sure
    so how could I compare
I try to find the emotions
    that explain just how I feel
The only one that comes to mind
    is guilt, I think its real
I thought I had the strength
    and could control my every thought
But I had a rude awakening
    I tried so hard for naught

THE MONARCH

The Monarch hung upon a branch
Safe in its snug cocoon
Thinking of its time of birth
That should happen some time soon

Emerging from its tight restraints
It burst forth in the sun
Breathing in the vastness
And the freedom it had won

It flew above a forest dense
Where trees below had grown
And touched some grain in fertile fields
That man one day had sown

It watched a child as she played below
Running from place to place
And heard her laugh and cry aloud
With a smile upon her face

Then before its bewildered eyes
The child began to age
And the playful lilt within her heart
Turned to an angry rage

The forest trees were gone for now
Her playground has turned to dust
She could not love as once she did
For now she could not trust

The Monarch flew in circles
Wondering where to go
What happened to this precious child?
This, it had to know

And then one day it saw her
Down in some city street
Walking with her head bowed low
Dragging her tired feet

She had searched, in vain, from day to day
To find that love once more
To rediscover her childlike self
Who had played some time before

But every time she caught a glimpse
And reached to grasp her tight
The little child would run away
And fade into the darkened night

The Monarch chased this lonely shadow
No smile upon its face
It could not find the child again
She left without a trace

MISSING DESIRES

There was a time, so long ago
    when life was such a joy.
"Twas not when I was grown to man,
    but just a little boy.

But somehow my very focus
    turned cloudy and ill-conceived;
I thought that life was good to me
    now I find I'd been deceived.

I thought I knew what mattered
    what was truly right and just.
I thought I knew what I had to do;
    my life was filled with trust.

But now I know how wrong I was
    my values changed so much.
Everything my mind had tried
    my soul just would not touch.

It wouldn't embrace the goodness
    I thought that I had found
Instead it chose despair and grief
    that hung silently around.

The sadness seems so heavy;
    it keeps me frozen still
It keeps my love from growing
    it saps my strength of will.

For longer than I remember
    I had it in my head,
That things would be so much better
    if only I were dead.

Now time goes by so slowly
    I care not what I do.
I wish I had some joy again
    and could begin my life anew.

RELEASING DESIRES

Often times I wondered why
    the days so slowly pass me by
I've done everything I thought I should
    and helped everyone I thought I could
I've lived the life of a righteous man
    and followed my predetermined plan
The road is steep, its rocky and its rough
    I'm tired! So tired, I've had enough!

I hope and pray for something new
    to enrich my days, my life renew,
I want my heart filled with love
    to hear the song of a distant dove.
My eyes to view the golden ray
    that brightens my life on a dreary day.
And, yet, of all the things I've tried
    I still sit numbly starry-eyed.

My spirit is dead from days gone past
    wearied by each worthless task
I want my mind freed from care;
    I want some joy that I can share;
I want to be loosed from society's grasp
    to unlock the grip of its binding clasp
For just a moment I experienced the thrill
    of the freedom of my new-found will
But it's gone for now - I'm sure forever;
    won't see it again...Never! No never!

RECOVERY

May your time in recovery
    bring strength every day.
May your Higher Power above
    show you a better way.
May your soul be full
    and overflowing with life.
May your path be clear
    and free from all strife.
May you find contentment
    to last you forever.
May you find only joy
    in your every endeavor.
May the love that you've found
    put hope in your heart.
May this new-found freedom
    be only the start.

CHOICES

My life is filled with grief;
    I'm wondering what to do.
I think of all my options;
    narrow them down to a few.
I can do what I've done before;
    not surrender to fate.
Or, I can change and try something new
    to save my life before its too late.

If I were standing on a cliff
    with only two ways to go down;
I could go straight ahead blindly
    and fall quickly to the ground.
Or, I can take the safer trail
    slowly to the ground below.
I can go very easy,
    and take it really slow.

The ideas I've had since I was small
    have brought me lots of grief.
They've stolen the freedom I had
    like some sneaky little thief.
They've kept me down in the pits of pity
    and crushed my dreams to dust.
The only way to change myself
    is to do what I know I must.

I have to take a look at myself,
Do I like what I see?
Is that the kind of person I am?
Is that really me?
Do I want to live my life
according to the dreams I've had?
Have they made me a worthwhile person,
or have they made me act this bad?

We all have faults I know,
and we all make some mistakes.
But to go on doing the same things wrong
makes us nothing but foolish fakes.
We keep this outside person
and hide the "real self"
And stick our full potential
high upon some cluttered shelf.

But there comes a time in my life of pain
when I don't like who I seem to be.
It's just some selfish person
it can't be really me.
It's then that I'll decide to change
and become a more loving soul.
I'll leave behind all the faults I had
and accept a more healthy role.

THE SEARCH IS ENDED

You have finally found
    a road to take
To lead you down
    to peaceful lake
To calm your mind
    with new serenity
To mold your soul
    with a new identity
To know exactly
    what you want to do
To find the true
    and only you.

A CHILD MUST GROW

I saw a child's smile;
    it beamed straight ahead my way.
It brightened a darkened moment,
    and lifted a lonely day.
The child's eyes were open
    to the wonders that he was seeing
Not knowing that later on in life
    from these wonders he would be fleeing.
What now seemed new and daring
    would later drag him down
Into the pits of Satan's hell;
    his smile would turn to frown.
The eyes that once were open
    would close and shut so tight;
To keep out the sun in daylight
    to keep out the moon at night.
The stars that twinkled brightly,
    as he dreamt of joys to come,
Would dim and die throughout the years
    and vanish one by one.
If only this child could stay as little
    as he was the day before,
He could cope with life the way it is;
    and want for nothing more.
But, alas, a child must grow
    and accept what comes his way.
He must live what he has been taught
    every single day.

CONTROLLING MY OWN DESTINY

I have to control my patience during times of frustration.
I have to control my depressions when I'm full of despair
I have to control my anger during times of confrontation.
I have to control my hate when no one seems to care.

These are some of the controls
　　that I need to find
To alter my style of life
　　to keep my peace of mind
I must constantly try to replace
　　old feelings with new
To change my way of thinking
　　to a healthier point of view
I'll care not how others
　　react to what I say
They'll not hurt my feelings
　　and direct my every day
I cannot feel sorry
　　for the situation I'm in
No guilt shall I have
　　every time that I sin
I might win my self-esteem
　　during chaotic discord
And find a richer, fuller life
　　as my final reward

THE REWARDS OF REMORSE

Although I see the sky above
    as a brilliant, azure blue,
And know how deep my truest love
    has always been for you.
I still can feel a twinge of pain
    every cold and lonely hour;
And from this sky, a burst of rain
    falls in a gentle shower.

My heart is saddened by things I've done
    and thoughts I wish I'd said,
As grotesque gray clouds cover sun
    above my low-bowed head.
The world is dim; its gray and dull
    with the passing of each moment.
Soft, sweet sounds - a sullen lull
    brings deep and bitter torment.

Despair is not so far away,
    it's closer than you think.
Creeping slowly day by day,
    causing me to sink.
I plummet down so very deep
    into filthy, dirty mire.
My only wish, that I could sleep,
    death is my desire.

At last I reach the bitter end,
    nowhere else to go.
The Dean of Death is sure to send
    his Prince to earth below.
And then, it will be over,
    comfort will come at last.
As dear friends sit and hover
    my loved one stands aghast.

DARKNESS AND DAWN

Darkness - black silhouette
　　　imperceptible shadows
Dawn - breathtaking sunrise
　　　an awakening of life

THE ENDLESS MERGER

The fine line between life and death is
like
the horizon between the earth and the sky.

One merges into the other endlessly - but

SUICIDE

The screaming crowd bellows in madness
   as the end draws very near.
The players dig deep down inside—
   confident, listening to every cheer.

No matter what the outcome
   they did the best they could.
They clawed, scraped and fought so hard,
   doing everything they thought they should.

The game nears finish, the score is tied
   and the pressure begins to rise.
Gnawing, foreboding tension builds;
   fear now fills the players eyes.

And then, for some, its over
   the game is done for sure.
These players lie in a huddled mass
   alone upon the barren floor.

Victory has elude others
   and crushed their lifelong hope.
It's left them lifeless, dangling;
   bound by a sturdy rope.

For death does take its toll
   and sets the spirit free.
It brings an end to a life of dreams,
   of something they could never be.

GROWTH AND PEACE OF MIND

Each time I reach out for help
    I find something new.
I find the support I need
    to begin my growth anew.
Every word and thought I hear
    helps stop my fall to hell.
I am better than I was before;
    this I'm proud to tell.

Conquering my despair
    was tough and very hard.
I had to live my life each day
    and be constantly on guard.
It caused me many problems
    it tore my soul apart.
But it's the only way I had to live
    I know this in my heart.

I'll find the strength I need
    to be proud of what I do.
I'll find the happiness
    that's been long since overdue.
I'll shed away my doubts and fears
    and the way I used to live.
I'll be a human being again
    and give all that I can give.

I'll know from day to day
    what I've done the day before.
I'll do things I'm proud to do,
    I'll search and I'll explore.
I'll be happy as I can be
    and I'll have fun every day.
I'll feel so good about myself,
    this is the only way.

I want to become a man,
    to grow and to mature.
I'll take whatever comes my way,
    I'll show I can endure.
I can survive every hardship
    without coming all apart.
I can step right back into my stride
    with a strong and happy heart.

I'll really know the difference
    from what is wrong and right.
I'll solve my problems every day
    and thank the Lord each night.
I'll think about my future
    and what I have to do.
I'll care and have the strength of will
    to follow my future through.

FREEDOM

FREEDOM!
   a piece of mind.
FREEDOM!
   no ties that bind.
FREEDOM!
   it's hard to find.

FREEDOM!
   to do what I must.
FREEDOM!
   to satisfy my lust.
FREEDOM!
   to live by trust.

FREEDOM!
   to improve my life.
FREEDOM!
   to relieve my strife.
FREEDOM!
   my only wife.

FREEDOM!
   to be forever free.
FREEDOM!
   to be only me.
FREEDOM!
   to be able to see.

The freedom I want
   will come some day
      somehow, sometime,
         somewhere, someway.

ACCEPTANCE

I accept whatever comes my way—
    good or bad, evil or just.
When I'm overwhelmed with troubles
    I stop and pray, and then adjust.

In times before I've struggled so;
    I've fought right to the end.
Now I find such calm content,
    as long as I can bend.

No matter that it gives me pain
    and tears my soul apart.
If I trust His will is best for me
    all my fears will soon depart.

To change my life I accept it all
    and live by faith alone.
I'll humble myself and with His help;
    I'll make it on my own.

THE JOURNEY

I surrender to the wonders
    of sight and smell and sound.
A blue sky, a fragrant flower,
    the song of a bird as
    as it wings it way around.

From its arboreal home it beckons,
    "Listen to my plaintiff cry.
Listen and hear my song of woe;
    help me live my life anew
    for soon I know I'll die."

And then, it flies in circles
    and searches for a place to land.
In mountains, in valleys, on ocean;
    as it washes its flotsam
    to yonder, waiting sand.

The wind howls its vengeance
    and whips him to and fro.
And where he'll rest his battered life
    he doesn't care
    and doesn't know.

With a sudden surge of inner peace
    he relents to the storm's raging fury.
He rides the currents ever calm
    no need to fight,
    no need to hurry.

And when the storm subsides in stillness
    and the sun dries the dampened earth
The bird will wake with life renewed,
    filled with hope
    of his emerging worth.

EXPECTATIONS

I expect this day to be
    better than the day before.
I expect it will turn out right
    to God I will implore.

I expect to live my life
    in a state of quiet bliss.
I expect my soul to be awakened
    by a gentle, loving kiss.

I expect a guiding hand
    to lead me through the briars.
I expect to fill my heart
    with all that it desires.

I expect I'll learn someday
    how to be a better man
I expect I'll find the answer
    when I take my final stand.

THE POWER OF ACCEPTANCE

I'm here in the present now,
    planning for tomorrow.
I'm preparing for my happiness
    to replace all my sorrow.
I'm laying out my path
    to be more than I am today.
I'm weighing every word
    that I think I ought to say.
I'm grasping for some strength
    to help me to endure.
I'm looking for some courage;
    right now I'm insecure.
I'm looking for the answers
    to change the ones I love.
I'm searching for serenity
    its somewhere up above.
Yet, I know that I can do
    about everything I could
And my life will work out
    just the way that it should.
I cannot force an outcome;
    I can only hope and pray;
I just accept what happens
    each and every day!

ANSWERING THE TELEPHONE

You are silent now. Everything is peaceful.
   There are no crises to be faced -
      something to smile about.

Nothing is happening. Everything is quiet.
   There are no feelings to be shared -
      nothing to lie about.

No one has been born. Everything is the same.
   My friends are still here -
      nothing to cry about.

Your silence is broken. Everything is changed.
   I hear all kinds of news -
      something to think about.

THE UPWARD STRUGGLE

I struggle toward the apex
    over a rocky, windy hill
I search for a new found freedom
    with peace and strength of will.

The road veers left
    and then veers right
And then it plummets
    out of sight.

Is the left foot first?
    or is it the right?
Do I travel by day?
    or maybe by night?

Each time I make progress
    I slide back twice as fast
I wish that I could forge ahead
    and leave behind my past.

The way is dark,
    its dreary, and its cold.
I seek some order in my life
    right now its uncontrolled.

I thought I had the power
    to control my every fate
But now its time to change my ways
    before its much too late.

But still I go on sinking
        my efforts fall so short
Now is the time to ask for help
        and reach for some support.

Slowly, very slowly
        I'm almost at the top.
I'll be very careful
        in case my climb should stop.

I could stop for just a while
        and catch my breath anew
But then I might begin to slip
        this I cannot do.

A TIME OF REFLECTION

Silence is a special gift.
I give it to myself when
I need freedom from all
the incessant chatter that
clutters my life.

It helps me speak to a
special friend whose
opinion I value most. I
speak to myself and I hear
what is truly in my heart.

I can argue back and forth
about what I've done wrong
so far. I can think about all
those tormenting moments
that caused me so much pain.

I can criticize every thought
that I could not utter aloud.
I can ease the burden I have
been carrying by admitting
that I am not perfect.

Silence gives me peace of
mind when everything around
is so hectic. It can help me
put my life in perspective even
though chaos surrounds me.

My silent hours bring cleansing
thoughts about my life and my
past. My silent moments give
me strength to do what I
really want to do.

But it is not easy at times
to grow in this silent way.
I find myself feeling lonely.
I become sad thinking about
the mistakes I have made.

From within this wall of silence
comes a revelation that I could
never before fathom. I cannot
change the past; I can only
change what I will do today.

My silence finally woke me
from my stupor. It brought
me to a dawn of new found
understanding. It took away
self-pity that I felt every day.

Silence is not as dreadful
as some people seem to feel.
Its just my way of meditating;
its just the way I pray.

GROWING OLD HOPELESSLY

The years pass by slowly at first,
    and then, as we lose our grip,
        faster and faster we begin to slip.

What was once a lively being,
    turns inward to feeble mind;
        reality quickly left behind.

Our confident gait deadens
    as we shuffle around;
        once erect bodies hunch closer to ground.

The furrows begin to deepen
    across our leathered face;
        it hardens and ashens at a frightening pace.

The twinkling in our eyes
    has diminished its glow;
        the toils of the years are beginning to show.

Our once nimble fingers
    become arthritic with pain;
        they stiffen and swell with each downpour of rain.

Our thoughts become hazy,
    we mumble each word;
        so very softly, barely to be heard.

Our time on earth is ending,
    or so we've been told;
        such is the fate of *hopelessly*
            growing old.

SERENITY

Like a misty haze creeping over
  silent, lonely vale

Like a wandering ship gliding under
  bleached, billowing sail

Like a solitary flower yawning amid
  mighty, statuesque trees

Like a fervent prayer in
  hushed, suppliant pleas

Like the sobering peace inside
  my aching, yearning heart

Like the golden glow in morning
  a new day begins
    and night will soon depart.

AWARENESS

I am aware of the world that surrounds me;
    the golden glow of light, the murmured hush of sound.
I am aware of what I love so much;
    the fragrant smells, the pleasures that I touch.

I am aware of the sun on high;
    its soothing warmth, its heated stare.
I am aware of a lover's smile;
    making me happy for a little while.

I am aware that I am aware;
    I yearn for life, I want, I care;
I am aware of where I was before;
    I want to be aware — to be aware
        for evermore.

FLEETING TIME

A friendly little nod
    to all who pass you by
Fills a heart with gladness
    if only you would try
But we cannot find the trust
    to give our love at will
To show our brothers friendship
    we lack that kind of skill
We ignore all these people
    who pass us by each day
We turn our heads away from friends
    who've helped along the way
Our eyes and ears are tightly closed
    to those who've gone astray
We think only of ourselves
    and what we do each day
Ease your mind a little
    enjoy the life around
Remember all the pretty things
    listen for every sound
Each moment is but a memory
    that ebbs quickly to the past
The days speed by so quickly
    they're over much too fast
The earth will spin forevermore
    but life on earth is brief
Remember all the fun you've had
    and forget your daily grief

CHANGE OF LIFE

I should love life for what its worth
   and give it all I've got.
For what I am deep down inside
   on the outside I sure am not.
By finding the good, the real me
   I can cope with all that's sent.
I can listen to what others say;
   and know just what is meant.

I want to know each day
   that peace lies just ahead.
I want to know that life on earth
   is better than being dead.
I want to know for sure,
   that someone really cares.
I want to feel the warmth and love
   of a friend who truly shares.

I just don't know what I can do
   to prove my worth anew.
I've bared my soul in sadness
   to a very precious few.
I've faced all the fears
   that paralyze my mind.
The answers to my confusion
   I try so hard to find.

I think I try too hard
        to do this on my own;
To live my life in peace and strength
        the way that I've been shown.
I've applied all the little tricks
        that keep my head up high.
I'll practice each and every day
        as my life slowly passes by.

Despite all my complex plans
        no simple way exists.
I must start right now, today;
        no second must I miss.
I will try because I care so much
        for loved ones and for me;
And maybe in the years ahead
        someday I will be free!

THE MIST

The lake before me isn't there. The white shadows
mask my view of the water, a distant island and the
mountains beyond. Just like the veil of doubt that
covers my mind and keeps me from the riches of
life, it clouds my very existence. Although I've
seen them before I cannot fathom what is beyond
the shadows. I cannot appreciate their beauty,
although I know it is there. The shadows forever
linger — teasing me, taunting me. And then,
through this curtain of haze a figure appears, glid-
ing silently forward. I can see it. It is truly there.
Then, suddenly it turns and fades back into the
mist, hidden from my view. Just like I doubt the
truths that exists. I need them always in front of
me.

A SUBJECT OF COMPROMISE

We travel together
　　you and I
Each down a separate road

Though you go left
　　and I go right
We'll meet somewhere in between

We travel together
　　you and I
And share a single load

THE GROWTH OF A FATHER

My baby!
    Are you crying?
        I should listen.
            I know what you need.

    Are you tired?
        I should leave.
            You should rest.

    Are you hungry?
        I should nourish you.
        I must feed you.

    Are you hurt?
        You can tell me.
            Where is the pain?

Shed your tears!
Raise your voice in wailing sobs!

My child!
    Are you crying?
        Should I listen?
            What do you want?

    Are you tired?
        Should I leave you?
            Should you be alone?

Are you hungry?
    Should I nourish you?
    Must I teach you?

Are you hurt?
    Can you tell me?
        What confuses you?

Shed your tears!
Raise your voice in pleading sighs!

My son!
    Are you crying?
    I will listen.
        I know what I've done

Are you tired?
    I will leave you.
        I will let you live.

Are you hungry?
    I will nourish you.
    I must free you.

Are you hurt?
    Don't tell me.
        I know what to do.

TAKE ACTION

Take action
    to set yourself free
        from what you've been taught

Forget the expectations
    that fill you with guilt
        when you cannot reach your goals

Dispel the fears
    of what people think
        as you make simple mistakes

Release the compulsion
    to be better than all
        as you strive for perfection

Be gentle with yourself
    as you do just what you can
        to be at peace with your life

ACCEPTING ACCEPTANCE

I can't understand acceptance;
    I wonder why it must be,
That all of these troubles
    should happen to me.

I feel that I'm worthless;
    but have I been that bad?
Did I deserve all the hardships
    and frustrations I've had?

I'll have to have faith
    that all will be right
If I could just let go;
    and give up my fight.

I'll have to accept life;
    this moment's so brief.
And enjoy all its beauty;
    and learn from its grief.

IN THE ROOMS OF THE FELLOWSHIP

I come to these rooms
    in my time of despair
When I've reached out for help
    and no one seemed to care

I come for the friendship
    and strength of their love
To help me find guidance
    from a Higher Power above

I come for my faith
    that's been lost for so long
I need it again
    to make me feel strong

I come to unburden
    my sorrow and my grief
To help ease my pain
    for life is too brief

I come to these rooms
    my heart in my hand
To share it with friends
    I know will understand

A LIGHT WILL SHINE

I want to reach the light above
    that keeps my hopes alive.
That gives me strength and courage
    that helps me to survive.

I'll survive because I'm worthy
    and deserve a whole lot more.
My self-esteem is better now
    that it was the day before.

There is no end to this search for light
    for there is no end to life.
It goes right on throughout the years,
    through sadness, grief, and strife.

It goes right on through gladness,
    and happiness and love.
While all the while I'm hoping
    to reach that light above.

If I try hard I'll find the strength
    to overcome despair
I'll find a friend who'll listen
    and be willing for me to share.

At times the light grows brighter
    reminding me that I'm not alone
I feel the peace and quiet
    that shows that I have grown.

I can seek the help of others
    who really want to care
And bask in the hands of love
    before I would not dare.

WE ARE ALWAYS TOGETHER

He's kind, he's gentle
    he's my special friend
I'm distraught, he consoles
    I'm rigid -- he helps me bend
I'm sad, he makes me smile
    I err, he corrects
I'm happy -- he shares my joy
    I fear, he protects

I live in the past
    he shows me the way
I'm lost in the future
    he brings me today
I'm angered by my faults
    he eases my frustration
I'm burdened by my duties
    he brings me liberation

I talk to him daily
    and seek his advice
He'll either nod yes
    or shake his head twice
He keeps all my thoughts
    flowing and free
For my special friend
    is none other than *me.*

THE VINE

Along the sleepy slopes,
Nestled among the resting hills
The vine stands barren now -
Its time has not yet come.

It hangs, wrinkled and withered,
Parched by a blazing sun;
With each gentle breeze it crackles,
It bends, it clings to existence.

The misty dawn awakens
The dormant seed ripens
The goodness within blossoms
It's time to begin to live

THE LAST FAREWELL

I wish I could understand the courage
you found to end your life that way. I
cannot imagine the pain you felt as you
woke each lonely day. I tried so hard to
tell you what would make life a better
place. Now, I only wish to hold you
and look into troubled your face. I
longed to sense a glow of hope radiate
from deep within your heart; to see a
smile embrace your lips -- as we hugged
and began to part. All I can do for now
is close my eyes to feel your special
love. I'll raise my head to see the clouds
that float lazily in the heavens above.
You'll help your God paint this sky with
blue and pale pink. You'll light each
evening with starlit hues as the sun
begins to sink.You'll place the moon into
an inky night with stars that twinkle
bright, as you stage a show for mom and
me while we dream of you each night.
It's time to say good-bye for now, though
I still feel ill at ease. I'll let you go; to
sail to heaven like a feather on a gentle
breeze.

A JOURNEY THROUGH RECOVERY

There is a road through recovery
It's there, just around the bend
If I walk a little faster
Maybe this road will end.

And if I do I'll reach my goal
My journey will be complete
Success will finally come my way
I will rise from my defeat.

But this road wanders forever
I'll travel it until my life expires
Each step I take brings me closer
To fulfill my souls desires.

It's the journey that gives me joy
It fills me with such content
It has shown me who I really am
It helps me love what God has sent.